YAS

FRIENDS

W9-AFQ-128

OF ACPL

SPORTS GREAT WAYNE GRETZKY

—*Sports Great Books*—

Sports Great Jim Abbott
(ISBN 0-89490-395-0)

Sports Great Troy Aikman
(ISBN 0-89490-593-7)

Sports Great Charles Barkley
(ISBN 0-89490-386-1)

Sports Great Larry Bird
(ISBN 0-89490-368-3)

Sports Great Barry Bonds
(ISBN 0-89490-595-3)

Sports Great Bobby Bonilla
(ISBN 0-89490-417-5)

Sports Great Will Clark
(ISBN 0-89490-390-X)

Sports Great Roger Clemens
(ISBN 0-89490-284-9)

Sports Great John Elway
(ISBN 0-89490-282-2)

Sports Great Patrick Ewing
(ISBN 0-89490-369-1)

Sports Great Steffi Graf
(ISBN 0-89490-597-X)

Sports Great Wayne Gretzky
(ISBN 0-89490-757-3)

Sports Great Orel Hershiser
(ISBN 0-89490-389-6)

Sports Great Bo Jackson
(ISBN 0-89490-281-4)

**Sports Great Magic Johnson
(Revised and Expanded)**
(ISBN 0-89490-348-9)

Sports Great Michael Jordan
(ISBN 0-89490-370-5)

Sports Great Mario Lemieux
(ISBN 0-89490-596-1)

Sports Great Karl Malone
(ISBN 0-89490-599-6)

Sports Great Kevin Mitchell
(ISBN 0-89490-388-8)

Sports Great Joe Montana
(ISBN 0-89490-371-3)

Sports Great Hakeem Olajuwon
(ISBN 0-89490-372-1)

Sports Great Shaquille O'Neal
(ISBN 0-89490-594-5)

Sports Great Kirby Puckett
(ISBN 0-89490-392-6)

Sports Great Jerry Rice
(ISBN 0-89490-419-1)

Sports Great Cal Ripken, Jr.
(ISBN 0-89490-387-X)

Sports Great David Robinson
(ISBN 0-89490-373-X)

Sports Great Nolan Ryan
(ISBN 0-89490-394-2)

Sports Great Barry Sanders
(ISBN 0-89490-418-3)

Sports Great John Stockton
(ISBN 0-89490-598-8)

Sports Great Darryl Strawberry
(ISBN 0-89490-291-1)

Sports Great Isiah Thomas
(ISBN 0-89490-374-8)

Sports Great Herschel Walker
(ISBN 0-89490-207-5)

SPORTS GREAT
WAYNE
GRETZKY

Ken Rappoport

—Sports Great Books—

ENSLOW PUBLISHERS, INC.

44 Fadem Road   P.O. Box 38
Box 699   Aldershot
Springfield, N.J. 07081   Hants GU12 6BP
U.S.A.   U.K.

For Griffin

Library of Congress Cataloging-in-Publication Data

Rappoport, Ken.
     Sports great Wayne Gretzky / Ken Rappoport
          p. cm.— (Sports great books)
     Includes index.
     Summary: A look at the personal life and hockey career of the player who was a star first
with the Edmonton Oilers and then with the Los Angeles Kings.
     ISBN 0-89490-757-3
     1. Gretzky, Wayne, 1961– —Juvenile literature. 2. Hockey
players—Canada—Biography—Juvenile literature. 3. Los Angeles
Kings (Hockey team)—Juvenile literature. [1. Gretzky, Wayne,
1961– . 2. Hockey players.] I. Title. II. Series
GV848.5.G73R37 1995
796.962'092—dc20
[B]   95-18840
                                                                                     CIP
                                                                                      AC

Illustration Credits: Brantford Expositor, pp. 14, 17, 19, 44; Doug Maclellan/
Hockey Hall of Fame, pp. 10, 35, 46, 53, 55, 58; Hockey Hall of Fame, pp. 20, 23, 26,
28, 34, 39, 56; L.A. Kings, pp. 42, 51; Miles Nadal/Hockey Hall of Fame, p. 37.

Cover Photo: Hockey Hall of Fame.

Contents

Chapter 1

"Hey, Phil, there's a kid here's gonna break your record some day."

"Yeah, who?"

"He's called Gretzky. Geez, Phil, what a kid."

—*Conversation between Phil Esposito and his father when Wayne Gretzky was sixteen and playing for the amateur Sault Ste. Marie Greyhounds of the Ontario Hockey League.*

Wayne Gretzky, "The Great One," skated onto the ice. Everyone wondered—would tonight be the night? Everyone was waiting.

Hunched over in his familiar, choppy skating style, the left side of his blue and orange jersey tucked into his pants, the Edmonton Oilers' star received an ovation. He slapped a practice shot past goaltender Grant Fuhr.

At 6 feet tall and 170 pounds, Gretzky is a frail figure in a violent team sport. Off the ice, he is dwarfed by his broad-shouldered teammates. On the ice, he stands head and shoulders above everyone else in the National Hockey League.

That winter night in 1982 in Buffalo, New York, there was more at stake than the outcome of the game.

The first period started. Excitement rippled through the crowd as Gretzky controlled the puck.

Gretzky had a "sixth sense" he had developed as a youngster. His dad taught him to see situations on the ice before everyone else. "Go where the puck is going. Anticipate, anticipate." Gretzky not only knew where everyone was on the ice, but where they were going to be.

Seeing an opportunity to score, he took a shot on net. The puck skittered weakly off his stick. Buffalo goaltender Don Edwards stopped it easily.

Gretzky, at the age of twenty-one, was on the verge of breaking the NHL's single-season goal record. Gretzky's blazing goal pace had excited the world of hockey. Hundreds of reporters followed the chase.

Three days earlier, Gretzky tied Phil Esposito's record of 76 goals in just his 63rd game of the season. It had taken 78 games for Esposito to establish the mark.

Now he needed just one goal to set the record.

In the second period, Gretzky blasted a twenty-five foot slapshot. Edwards stuck out his glove and snapped the puck out of the air.

Moments later, Gretzky stickhandled through a mass of swirling players. He backhanded a quick shot at Edwards. He was stopped, once again.

Edwards was a tough opponent for Gretzky. An All-Star goaltender and former teammate on the Canadian team that played in the Canada Cup, Edwards had allowed Gretzky only one goal in three seasons.

That night in Buffalo, it looked as if the trend would continue.

It was late in the second period. About thirty feet away from the net in center ice, Gretzky unleashed a slapshot.

Edwards tensed. The puck smacked into the goaltender's pads and skidded away.

As Gretzky neared the record, the pressure mounted. Esposito attended each game, waiting for the big goal. NHL president John Ziegler joined the group following Gretzky. Gretzky was attacked with questions about the record. When would it happen? Where would it happen? A stress-filled Gretzky hoped he could live up to everyone's expectations.

Early in the third period, Gretzky broke away from the Buffalo defense. He skated in alone and blasted a sizzling shot on net that seemed impossible to stop.

As the crowd of 16,433 held its breath, Edwards made a spectacular, diving save.

No goal!

Could Gretzky do it? There were less than seven minutes left in the game. Gretzky had had four excellent chances but had been stopped each time by Edwards.

Gretzky was visibly tired and under tremendous pressure. He bent over, leaning forward on his knees to get a second wind. He wanted to break that record, more than anything.

With the score tied 3–3, suddenly Buffalo right wing Steve Patrick lost control of the puck. Gretzky pounced on the puck with the Buffalo defense breathing down his neck.

Just then, Gretzky spied a slip of open ice. That's all he needed. Faking out his defenders, skating this way and that, Gretzky broke clear and headed for the net with the Sabres in hot pursuit.

Now open space loomed between Gretzky and the Sabres' goaltender. Before the sellout crowd seemed to realize it, Gretzky exploded across the ice and slammed a 10-foot wrist shot past Edwards with 6 minutes and 36 seconds remaining.

Goal number 77!

Gretzky's teammates flooded off the bench, surrounding

At the age of twenty-one, "The Great One" surpassed Phil Esposito's record of 76 goals in one season.

him while the crowd applauded and gave him a standing ovation. The game stopped. In a short ceremony, Esposito presented Gretzky with the record-breaking puck.

"My first thought was that it put us ahead," Gretzky later said of the record-breaking goal. "Then, as I turned to stride to the corner, I felt relief and satisfaction. It's a lot of pressure off me."

Gretzky scored two more goals in the final two minutes to give the Oilers a 6–3 victory.

With sixteen games left in the season, how many more would The Great One score?

Not a bad year for someone who was supposed to be "washed up" by the time he reached adolescence.

Chapter 2

It was long past sundown and suppertime. Fierce winter winds howled out of the Canadian north. For a group of boys in Brantford, Ontario, it was a perfect time for hockey.

Scarfs protected their necks and faces from the bitter cold as they skated tirelessly around the ice, wiping runny noses with their sleeves. They played late into the night, until their parents came to take them home. They left grudgingly.

Wayne Gretzky was always the last to leave. His parents had to drag him off the ice to do household chores or homework. Wayne bribed his friends with nickels so they would stay longer at his backyard rink.

The rink was the idea of Wayne's father, Walter. When the grass froze, he flooded the yard with water. It was a good size for boys' hockey—about sixty by forty feet.

As a boy, Wayne's whole life centered around the backyard rink. It was his own field of dreams. Day or night, Wayne was there. Sometimes he played alone under the light of lamps and a sky of stars. Then he pretended to be one of his hockey heroes—Gordie Howe, Frank Mahovlich, Boom Boom Geoffrion.

"He shoots . . . he scores!" Gretzky could hear in his mind the booming voice of Foster Hewitt, the well-known professional hockey broadcaster.

Wayne imagined he was on the ice at the Montreal Forum or the Maple Leaf Gardens in Toronto, two of the most famous arenas in hockey.

Hockey is a fast, violent game. There are six players on each team—five skaters and one goaltender to guard the net. Three forwards (right wing, left wing, and center) play up front and two defensemen play at the rear. Players use their sticks to push the puck along the ice. They pass to teammates to set up scoring opportunities. A goal is counted if the puck goes into the net. The opposing goaltender, using his or her large glove, body, feet, or stick, tries to keep the puck out.

While on his rink, Wayne played a solitary game called "Rush." He used his hockey stick to push the puck along the ice. The puck that is used in hockey is a hard, black rubber disc that looks like a large Oreo™ cookie without the cream in the middle.

Pushing the puck from the far end of the ice, Wayne rushed and picked up speed. With the apple-red goalposts in his sights, he unleashed a hard shot.

The puck sizzled along the ice and nestled in the net.

It was a tricky course for Wayne to maneuver. His father placed tin cans, pylons (traffic cones), and hockey sticks on the ice. Wayne skillfully skated around or jumped over them. He controlled the puck as if it were attached to his stick. It was fun having his own obstacle course.

Soon he was able to jump over a stick and flip the puck at the same time. He felt good when the puck went into the net.

Although Wayne loved all sports as a boy, hockey was

Wayne loved all sports as a boy. Here, he is in a hockey uniform holding a lacrosse stick at the age of ten.

always a constant in his life. At Christmas, his parents always bought him the same present—a net. "They didn't last too long," Walter Gretzky said. "Every Christmas, he looked forward to hockey nets. He never bothered with toys or guns as a little boy."

Hockey was a natural way of life for Wayne Gretzky, who was born on January 26, 1961, in Brantford, a Canadian town of 78,000 people, about 60 miles from Toronto.

Every Saturday night, the family gathered at his grandfather's farm outside Brantford to watch "Hockey Night in Canada." Wayne imitated the players he saw on television. He slid around the pine floor and knocked a sponge ball into the "goal posts"—his grandmother's legs.

The farm was Wayne's favorite place. Wayne spent most weekends there. He skated on the scenic Nith River in the winter. He fished and played baseball in the summer. When he grew up and became famous, Wayne went back to the farm for quiet weekends.

Wayne's father had been an amateur hockey player. He worked for a telephone company as an installer repairman. Like many Canadian parents, Walter and Phyllis Gretzky encouraged their children in sports—not that Wayne needed encouragement.

Sports are filled with father-and-son relationships. Few were better than the one between Wayne and Walter Gretzky. Walter Gretzky was always there to support his son and give him needed advice. And, when the situation required it, Walter also supplied the humor.

As a young boy, Wayne once lost three front teeth in a hockey game. On his way to the hospital, an upset Wayne sat in the front seat of his father's car.

Looking at the clownish hole in his son's teeth, Walter quipped: "Well, at least you look like a hockey player."

At the age of two, Wayne took to skates the way a penguin takes to ice. The oldest of four brothers, Wayne led the way for Keith, Glen, and Brent. Wayne's sister, Kim, would later become a track star.

Wayne was four years old when his father put up the hockey rink in the backyard. Because his son was so small, Walter Gretzky found him the smallest hockey stick available. He sized it down so Wayne could get a better grip.

At five, Wayne tried out for the local youth hockey team. He was turned away—too young.

Wayne was disappointed. He wanted to play on a team. There was only one thing to do—go home and practice.

Wayne had great determination. His father said, "Whenever he decided he wanted to do something, he would do it no matter how long it took."

The following year, six-year-old Wayne went back for another tryout. Kids up to ten years old were trying out. He looked lost among all the bigger players.

Wayne was determined not to be sent home again. He was not going to let his age, or his size, stop him. Wayne impressed the coaches with his skating and puck-handling skills. He made the team.

Wayne was proud to be a member of the Brantford Nadrofsky Steelers. When Wayne scored his only goal of the year, his teammates surrounded him. Wayne was so small he could not be seen by the crowd.

Five years later he couldn't be missed.

When Wayne turned eleven in the 1971–72 season, he scored an astounding 378 goals. He received national attention in Canada and resentment from jealous parents of other hockey players.

They shouted insults at him when he was on the ice. "Hot dog . . . puck hog."

Wayne started playing on hockey teams when he was six years old. Though he was smaller than most of the other players, he was a valuable addition to the Brantford Nadrofsky Steelers.

Because Wayne started playing at an early age, and was getting so much ice time, people predicted he would be "washed up" by the time he was twelve. Playing two games a day in different towns was not unusual for Wayne.

Before long, Wayne didn't have to worry about jealous parents in small-town Brantford. He was on his way to big-city Toronto. There, in a more advanced league, he could play against some of the best young players in Canada.

For the first time in his life, Wayne would be living away from home. You can imagine how difficult this was for a fourteen-year-old and how hard a decision it was for his family. But Wayne and his parents thought it would be best for him to get away from his goldfish-bowl existence in Brantford. "I moved away just to escape all the pressures parents [not his own] place on kids," Gretzky said in later years. "It's not kids against each other, it's the parents."

In Toronto, Wayne lived with a family interested in his hockey career. He was homesick—but only when he wasn't playing with the Toronto Young Nationals of the Metro Junior B Hockey League.

Wayne had become a skinny teenager who barely weighed 135 pounds. Most of the players in the league were bigger and older, some as old as twenty. Some of Wayne's teammates were married and had families. Wayne wasn't even old enough to have a driver's license.

Once again, Wayne found himself to be the youngest and smallest player on the ice. And once again, it didn't matter.

Wayne was rookie of the year in the Metro League. In two years, Wayne graduated to the Sault Ste. Marie Greyhounds, who played in one of Canada's best amateur leagues.

In his first game with the Greyhounds, Wayne had 3 goals and 3 assists. Wayne was "on a real high" and anxious to

Wayne often played more than one game a day in different towns when he was young. Many thought this would wear him out, but he proved his doubters wrong.

share his excitement with his father. One look at his father's face stopped him dead in his tracks.

"The goals and assists mean nothing," Walter Gretzky said firmly to his son. "You stood around and let everyone else do the work."

It was a lesson Wayne never forgot.

With the Greyhounds, Gretzky picked a number that became forever linked to his name.

Wayne had worn No. 9, the same number worn by his idol, Gordie Howe. But when he arrived in Sault Ste. Marie, No. 9 was taken.

Someone suggested Gretzky wear No. 99. But such a high number was uncommon in hockey. Wayne thought it would just be an open invitation for players to target him.

"They'll run at you anyway," a friend told Gretzky.

Gretzky took the number.

At Sault Ste. Marie, Wayne Gretzky became a bigger

celebrity. His teammates called him "Ink." He was constantly in the newspapers.

Gretzky received attention from professional teams. At seventeen he was underage for the National Hockey League (NHL). The rival World Hockey Association (WHA), a new league battling the older, established NHL for players, didn't care how young he was. The WHA needed a big name like Gretzky to sell itself.

Thus Gretzky, the greatest junior player in Canada, signed

When Wayne Gretzky began to play with the Greyhounds, his favorite number, No. 9, was taken. He decided to wear No. 99 instead—the number would forever be linked with his name.

with the Indianapolis Racers instead of an NHL team. He was flying high when he signed his first contract—in the private jet of the Racers' owner. The four-year deal was worth $1.7 million.

Wayne Gretzky always looked like a million dollars on the ice. Now he was a millionaire for real.

Chapter 3

Wayne Gretzky was sitting and suffering.

The star of every league, Gretzky suddenly found himself on the bench. Watching more than playing, he was frustrated.

Gretzky was only seventeen and Indianapolis Racers coach Pat "Whitey" Stapleton was afraid to rush him along in a league of hardened professionals. The coach cut his ice time.

Gretzky's performance fell off. People started doubting his ability. "The pressure was tougher on him [the way Stapleton was using him]," said Gretzky's dad. "Wayne was expected to perform. When he did get on the ice, he scored."

The media wrote that Wayne Gretzky could not skate well enough for the professional teams. He wouldn't last long.

That's all Gretzky had to hear. "I'll prove them wrong," he said.

He did. But not until he was a member of the Edmonton Oilers. After only eight games with Indianapolis, Wayne Gretzky was sold to the Oilers by the cash-strapped Racers. He played more, especially after showing coach Glen Sather he was mentally tough.

Gretzky found himself on the bench again after a poor defensive play cost the Oilers a goal against the Cincinnati Stingers. When Sather put Gretzky back in, it was the third period and the Oilers trailed 2–1.

"That to me was the turning point in his pro career," Sather said. "He could have pouted and sulked."

Gretzky scored 3 goals, leading the Oilers to a 5–2 victory. He wound up scoring 46 goals for the season and winning the Rookie-of-the-Year Award in the WHA.

An unusual eighteenth birthday present from Oilers' owner Peter Pocklington highlighted Wayne's first season in professional hockey: a new twenty-one-year contract at the then staggering sum of about $300,000 a year. Pocklington had a flair for the dramatic. The contract—the longest in professional sports—would run until '99, matching Gretzky's uniform number.

The Oilers joined the National Hockey League the

When Gretzky turned eighteen, the Edmonton Oilers offered him a twenty-one year contract. The contract would expire in the year '99—the same number as his uniform.

following season and Gretzky began hearing that same old ˈ refrain: too young, too frail, too slow.

With his relatively thin frame, the 160-pound Gretzky was considered a lightweight when compared to many of the larger players in the NHL. The critics were not impressed with his speed or his shot.

The WHA was recognized as an inferior league to the NHL. Let's see Gretzky do the same thing in the stronger NHL, his critics said.

Once again, Gretzky was determined to prove himself.

Gretzky's goal: score as many points in his first season in the NHL as he did in the WHA (110). He did better. He tied for the league-scoring championship (137). He won the Hart Trophy (most valuable player) and the Lady Byng Trophy (most gentlemanly player).

Gretzky not only wanted to prove his critics wrong, he seemed in a hurry to do it.

When he turned twenty-one, he scored 92 goals to break Phil Esposito's single-season record of 76. That same season, he became the first player to score 200 points. A player's point total is determined by adding up his goals and assists. A player gets an assist if he helps set up a teammate for a goal. In the 1981–82 season, Gretzky had 92 goals and 120 assists for 212 points.

First came a 200-point season—and then, The Streak.

At first, no one thought much about it. Gretzky started scoring at the start of the 1983–84 season. When he scored in every one of the first 31 games, everyone began to take notice. Gretzky had broken his own NHL point-scoring streak and seemed to be on a determined mission.

By the time his streak had climbed into the 40-game range, the media had climbed aboard the Gretzky bandwagon.

As the streak mounted, so did the number of sportswriters following The Great One.

Could he score in every game that season? It hardly seemed possible. But, then again, this was Wayne Gretzky—hockey's wonder boy.

Unlike baseball star Roger Maris, who lost his hair during his 1961 assault on Babe Ruth's home run record, Gretzky hardly thought about the continuing pressure.

"I felt a little pressure to break 30, but after that I just said, 'Hey, this is fun. I wonder how long it can last?'"

It lasted 51 games. The Streak was finally broken.

Gretzky missed the next six games with a shoulder injury. He returned to score in 20 of the remaining 22 games. In one of the most astounding performances in hockey history, Gretzky played 74 games that season and was held scoreless only three times!

The Streak was one of the big stories of the 1983–84 season. Another was the Edmonton Oilers team, a rising power in the NHL with a core of great young players.

The Oilers' version of the "baby boom" was about to explode in the NHL. With such players as Wayne Gretzky, Mark Messier, Jari Kurri, and Paul Coffey, they seemed ready to challenge the powerful New York Islanders, who had won four straight Stanley Cups from 1980–83.

The Oilers had served notice in the 1981 playoffs when they knocked out Montreal in the first round, then gave the Islanders their toughest series.

The Oilers still had a long way to go to be champions. They were a brash, young team and lacked the discipline needed to put them over the top. As youngsters do, they didn't listen when the coaches told them what needed to be done. They went out and did things their way—and often lost the crucial games.

"The Streak"—Gretzky scored points 51 games in a row in the 1983–84 season.

In 1982 they were beaten by an inferior Los Angeles team in the playoffs. The Oilers had finished with the second-best record during the regular season, behind the Islanders.

"We weren't ready to win, we weren't mature enough," Gretzky said.

There was no love lost between the Oilers and Islanders. The Oilers had irritated the Islanders with their youthful enthusiasm. Sitting on the bench, cheering themselves, they chanted, "Here we go, Oilers, here we go!"

"Everybody showed their feelings in those days," said Edmonton defenseman Kevin Lowe. "We were kids, we were striving to be known and struggling for respect. And we were just having fun. People took it in the wrong sense."

In 1983 the Islanders embarrassed the Oilers by winning four straight games in the finals.

In 1984 the Oilers wanted revenge. The Islanders had great veteran players like Mike Bossy, Denis Potvin, Billy Smith, and Bryan Trottier. Could the young, upstart Oilers finally unseat the Islanders, who were considered one of the greatest dynasties in NHL history?

In the first game of the finals, Islander goaltender Billy Smith was at his best. Grant Fuhr was better for Edmonton. Final: Oilers 1, Islanders 0.

Game Two belonged to the Islanders, 6–1. The best-of-seven series moved to Edmonton for the next three games with the teams tied at 1 1.

In both games on Long Island, Gretzky was not at his best. He was held without a point in a sudden bewildering slump.

The third game wasn't much better for The Great One, even though the Oilers won, 7–2. For the third straight game, Gretzky—who had scored 87 goals during the regular season—was held without a goal.

How much longer would his slump continue? Even

Although he had scored 87 goals during the regular season, Gretzky was unable to score one during the first three games of the Stanley Cup series in 1984.

though the Oilers were leading the series, Gretzky wanted to contribute to their success.

Less than two minutes into the first period of Game Four, Gretzky went in on a breakaway to give the Oilers a 1–0 lead and end his goalless streak. He later scored the game's final goal. The Oilers beat the Islanders 7–2 and moved one game away from their first Stanley Cup.

Gretzky knew the Oilers still had a lot of work to do against a proud, powerful opponent.

"If we think we've won it, we're in trouble," Gretzky said.

Gretzky dearly wanted to win the Cup in Edmonton, and not only for the Oiler fans. He didn't want his team to have to go back to Long Island and play the Islanders in their home rink. He preferred a victory parade in Edmonton rather than making another long flight back to New York. He hated flying. It scared him. On the Oilers' flights, Gretzky could often be seen sitting in the cockpit with the pilots. Somehow, he felt safer there.

The Oilers started Game Five fast as Gretzky scored twice. Shaking off a New York defender who had shadowed him from the beginning, Gretzky took a pass from Jari Kurri and scored.

Once again, Gretzky teamed with Kurri to score again: 2–0, Edmonton.

With Gretzky assisting on another goal, the Oilers took a 4–0 lead after two periods. Only twenty minutes to go and the Oilers would be Stanley Cup champions.

But the Islanders scored two goals in the first thirty-five seconds of the third period to cut the Oilers' lead to 4–2.

There was still 19 minutes and 25 seconds left to play—plenty of time for the Islanders to come back.

But the Oilers weren't about to let that happen. The Oilers

had relaxed with a four-goal lead. Now they tightened their defense. Instead, it was New York who gave up the final goal.

The final score was: Oilers 5, Islanders 2.

The game-ending buzzer set off pandemonium in the Northlands Coliseum. The Oilers hugged each other as big, multicolored balloons flooded the ice. Thousands of fans joined in the celebration.

"There's no feeling like this, nothing compares," said Gretzky, who skated around the Edmonton rink with tears in his eyes and his twelve-year-old brother, Brent (who later played in the NHL), on his shoulders. "The best thing about winning? We don't have to read in the papers again that the Oilers haven't won anything."

Now that the Oilers had won their first Stanley Cup, could they keep it going?

Chapter 4

The sign said it all: "Edmonton—City of Champions."

The Canadian city with the long, snowy winters had boasted literally hundreds of internationally recognized champions from the world-beating Edmonton Grads women's basketball team to world-reknown figure skaters. Now the Edmonton Oilers of the National Hockey League had joined the championship circle.

Like Edmonton, a relatively young city in Canada's flat western plains, the Oilers were a team coming of age.

Edmonton was a boomtown founded on oil and cattle, like the American West. Now the Oilers had become another precious natural resource. At the center was Wayne Gretzky, who was making 200-point seasons a regularity and keying the most explosive offense in hockey history.

The Oilers took aim on their second Cup when they faced the Philadelphia Flyers in the 1985 finals.

The Flyers were one of the best defensive teams in the league and had an eight-game unbeaten streak against the

Oilers. The championship series figured to be a classic matchup: offense vs. defense.

If the Oilers needed a good, swift kick in the pants, they got it. Defense won the opening game as the Flyers kept Wayne Gretzky from getting a single shot on goal, and beat the Oilers 4–1.

The determined Oilers came back to win Game Two, 3–1, as Gretzky scored one goal.

Game Three opened in Edmonton. Gretzky was determined to let loose before the hometown fans.

As the fans were settling into their seats, Gretzky showed why he was the most dangerous scorer in hockey.

Gretzky took Jari Kurri's pass in the right wing faceoff circle and skated around a Flyers' forward. Faking goaltender Pelle Lindbergh to the ice, he slipped a backhander into the net for a 1–0 Oilers lead.

Fifteen seconds later, Gretzky deflected a pass from Paul Coffey into the net to make it 2–0.

All in the first one hundred seconds.

Later in the period, Gretzky cut in front of the net when a teammate's pass found his stick. He snapped in a wrist shot for his third goal.

It was the first time that season the Flyers had allowed an opponent to score three goals in a game—and Gretzky had done it in one period!

Gretzky assisted on another goal as the Oilers won 4–3.

Gretzky felt the Oilers' confidence grow. "We're two wins away from the Stanley Cup and can smell it."

Tied 3–3 in Game Four, the Oilers won 5–3 as Gretzky scored twice. Now they were one win closer.

In Game Five, the Oilers rushed to an early 4–1 lead and steadily built their advantage. With two minutes left, the exhuberant crowd chanted, "The Cup stays here!" It did, as the Oilers won, 8–3.

"We've got the reputation of being an arrogant, flash-in-the-pan type of team, so we didn't want to win one Cup and not win another," Gretzky said after a playoff-record performance (17 goals and 30 assists).

In the jubilant Edmonton Oilers' locker room, drenched with champagne, forward Mike Krushelnyski, exclaimed "Unbelievable!"

He was talking not only about his first Stanley Cup, but also about the Great Gretzky.

"You'll be in a place where you figure there's no possible way Wayne can get you the puck. Then, all of a sudden, he's got the pass over to you. You've always got to be prepared."

When the 1985–86 season started, the Oilers were favored to win their third Cup. They finished with the best record in the NHL, losing only 17 games in an 80-game schedule.

It was said the only team that could beat the Oilers were the Oilers themselves.

It was the semifinals of the 1986 playoffs. The Oilers faced their arch-rivals, the Calgary Flames, in the deciding seventh game at Edmonton.

The score was tied, 2–2, in the third period. Oilers defenseman Steve Smith, standing behind the goal line, was about to carry the puck out of his own end.

Smith looked up ice to see which of his Oiler teammates was clear for the pass. He hesitated for a moment, then shot.

Oilers goaltender Grant Fuhr, like everyone else, was looking up ice when he got the surprise of his life.

Something hard hit the back of his skate. To the dismay of the Edmonton fans, Smith's pass had been deflected by goalie Fuhr's skate into the Oilers' own net.

Gretzky holds the Stanley Cup high above his head. Winning it became a habit in Edmonton.

Everyone was shocked. The bizarre goal gave the visiting Flames a 3–2 lead. The Oilers never recovered.

When the Oilers reclaimed the Cup in 1987 with a victory over Philadelphia, Smith was the second player to carry the Stanley Cup around the ice. As captain, Gretzky carried the Cup first. Then he made sure to give it to Smith—a grand gesture. As Smith raised the Cup over his head in celebration, it erased a year of pain.

Wayne Gretzky (left) and Grant Fuhr congratulate each other after another victory. This time, they were playing for team Canada.

The Oilers now had won three Stanley Cups in four years. Was another championship in the cards in 1988?

Gretzky, who suffered a knee and eye injury, missed eighteen games of the 1987–88 season and didn't win the scoring title for the first time in eight years. With The Great One missing, the Oilers failed to win their division championship and slipped to the third-best record in the NHL.

Gretzky's mid-season rest actually worked to the Oilers' advantage. He was fresh for the playoffs when they started the defense of their league championship.

After beating Winnipeg in the first round, the Oilers faced Calgary, the team that had knocked them out of the playoffs two years before.

The first game featured a defensive battle between the rivals. Gretzky's breakaway goal late in the third period clinched a 3–1 victory for the Oilers.

In Game Two the Oilers rallied from a two-goal deficit to send the contest into overtime. In hockey, the first team to score during overtime wins the game. For six minutes, the arch-rivals battled back and forth, neither side giving an inch.

Then a penalty left the Oilers shorthanded. Gretzky was sent out on the ice with the penalty-killing unit.

Before the Flames knew what had hit them, Kurri fired a pass to Gretzky along the boards. Gretzky streaked in on the Flames' net and rifled a shot past Calgary goaltender Mike Vernon: Goal, Oilers win!

The loss seemed to break the spirit of the Flames. The Oilers completed a sweep with two victories at home.

In a rugged semifinal series, the Oilers beat Detroit to advance to the finals against Boston. With Gretzky at the top of his game, the Oilers swept the Bruins in four straight, including a 6–3 victory in the final game. Gretzky set records in the finals: 10 assists and 13 points. He was named the Most

Wayne Gretzky led the Edmonton Oilers to four championships within five years, making the team a dynasty.

Valuable Player as the Edmonton Oilers won their fourth Cup in five years.

In sports, a dynasty is considered a team that wins at least three straight championships or dominates for a long period. With Gretzky as the leading player, the Oilers had earned the right to be called a dynasty.

But was the foundation of this dynasty about to be broken apart? Rumors were circulating: Gretzky was about to be traded by the Oilers.

They were true.

It came as a shock to Gretzky. He had received a call while on his honeymoon with actress Janet Jones informing him that Oilers owner Peter Pocklington had him on the market. Hurt and angry, Gretzky called his dad.

"My dad tried to get me to calm down," Gretzky said, "but I told him I had already made up my mind I was never going to wear an Oilers uniform again."

"How can you go on playing for an organization when the day after you win the Stanley Cup, they are trying to trade you?"

The Oilers called a "major press conference" for the morning of August 8, 1988. About two hundred reporters gathered for the big event.

The Oilers dropped the bombshell.

They had traded Gretzky to the Los Angeles Kings. Included in the $15 million trade were four players and three draft picks.

A solemn Gretzky seemed as if he would rather be in the penalty box than face the media on this day.

Speaking without notes, he began to express his thanks to the people of Edmonton, a town he had put on the hockey map. Tearful, he struggled to talk.

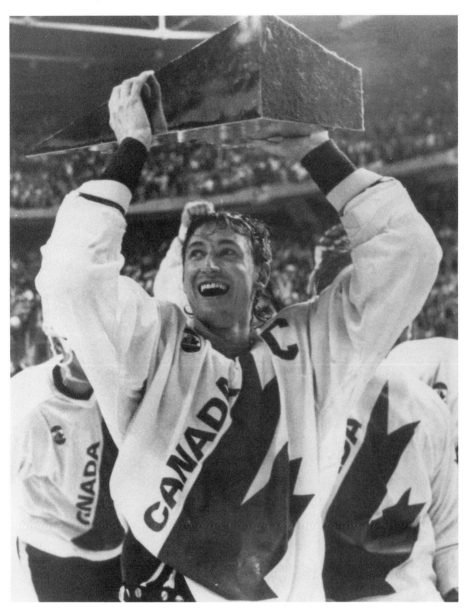

Gretzky was hurt and angry when, immediately after he helped his team win the Stanley Cup, the Oilers' owner traded him to the Los Angeles Kings. Neither the fans nor Gretzky understood the decision. Here, Gretzky lofts the Canada Cup after winning the international tournament in 1987.

"It's disappointing having to leave Edmonton . . . there comes a time when . . . "

He stopped, unable to go on.

It was unbelievable! The Oiler fans considered him a national treasure. A member of the Canadian Parliament had urged government intervention to stop the trade. "The Edmonton Oilers without Wayne Gretzky is like winter without snow," he said. "It's quite unthinkable."

Gretzky arrived in Los Angeles hailed as a "franchise saver" for a team with an unsuccessful history. In their twenty-two years, the Kings had never advanced to the Stanley Cup finals.

Could just one man, even if he was the Great Gretzky, change the course of the Kings' future?

Chapter 5

The stage was set.

Hockey, the Sleeping Beauty of Hollywood, was about to be awakened by a King. Anticipation flooded Los Angeles.

Tickets were in high demand for the opportunity to witness the debut of the Los Angeles Kings' newest star, Wayne Gretzky.

In a place more accustomed to surfing than skating, hockey fever had suddenly gripped southern California.

For the first time in their history, the Kings had a sellout on opening night. The upscale audience included many Hollywood celebrities. Sitting behind the Kings bench were John Candy, Michael J. Fox, and Goldie Hawn. Other celebrities were scattered throughout the crowd anticipating the appearance of Wayne Gretzky. Ten times the normal number of sportswriters recorded the event.

An Edmonton sportswriter had written that it was a shame to waste Gretzky on Southern Californians because they "didn't love hockey or hate it . . . just didn't pay any attention."

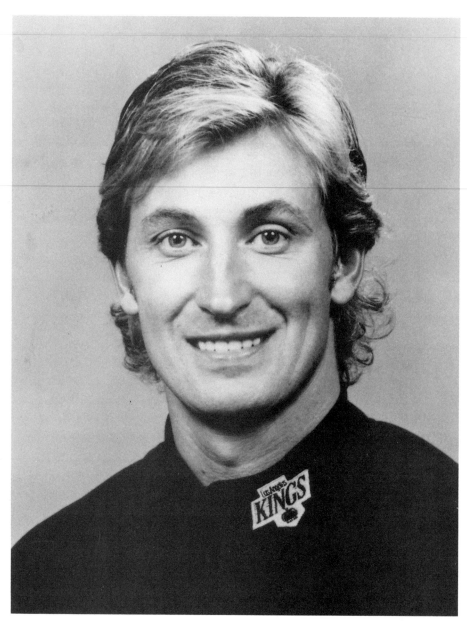

The pressure was on Gretzky when he joined the L.A. Kings. Could "The Great One" rouse interest in a sport that was of no interest to many Los Angeles residents? Could he carry a team to the Stanley Cup finals that hadn't been there in all of its history?

They were paying attention now.

The arena darkened. The spotlight was on center ice as the Kings were introduced one by one to the cheers of the 16,005 at the Los Angeles Forum. Finally, the familiar No. 99 on a black and silver jersey glided onto the rink to greet his new teammates. As applause and cheers rocked the building, Gretzky dashed off for a warm-up skate.

Would Gretzky be able to bring the Kings to life?

In the first period, the Kings were down one goal but had a two-man advantage and were circling in front of the Detroit Red Wings' net, looking for an opening.

Dave Taylor spotted Gretzky down low at the side of the net. He fired a sharp pass that crossed in front.

Gretzky flicked the puck past Red Wings goaltender Greg Stefan at 12 minutes and 54 seconds to tie the game at 1–1.

Thunderous cheers shook the Forum. The show was on.

Gretzky assisted on three other goals, leading the Kings to an 8–2 rout of the Red Wings.

"I don't think they would have dominated us without Gretzky," Red Wings coach Jacques Demers said. "I haven't seen a Kings team play like that in a long time. Gretzky makes every one of them better."

The Gretzky Era in Los Angeles was underway. And now, wearing a Kings uniform, Gretzky was closing in on one of hockey's most impressive achievements: Gordie Howe's all-time National Hockey League points record. Howe was a player many considered the greatest ever to play the game.

For Wayne Gretzky, the points record had more than the usual significance.

It all began when Gretzky was a young boy.

At the age of eleven, Gretzky had attended a sports awards banquet that featured a variety of stars including Howe.

Gretzky was unexpectedly called to the microphone to say

At age eleven, Wayne Gretzky met his idol, Gordie Howe (left). At age twenty-seven, Gretzky was closing in on Howe's all-time National Hockey League points record.

a few words. Suddenly, in front of his awe-inspiring audience, the words wouldn't come out.

Seconds seemed like an eternity as the dumbfounded Gretzky stood there. Jumping out of his seat, Howe raced to Gretzky's side, put his arm around the frightened young man, and grabbed the mike.

"When someone has done what this kid has done in the rink, he doesn't have to say anything," Howe said.

The audience broke into applause. Gretzky could not stop blushing.

Gretzky and his idol posed for a picture. Howe gave Gretzky some advice: "Work on your backhand."

That advice proved valuable as Gretzky continued his assault on Howe's scoring record.

Coming into the 1988–89 NHL season, Gretzky had 1,837 points—just 13 behind Howe's record of 1,850.

Now, as Gretzky approached the record, Howe was traveling with the Kings. In the third game of the season, Gretzky had 3 assists against the Detroit Red Wings.

Two days later, Gretzky had 1 goal and 2 assists against the New York Islanders.

Now he was only 5 points from the record.

Against Vancouver, he added 3 more points, including an assist on the game-winning goal.

There were only 2 points to go.

On the night of October 15, 1989, Gretzky returned to the Northlands Coliseum in Edmonton to face his former teammates. Would he break Howe's record in Edmonton?

Playing against the Oilers would be emotional. Gretzky had played for ten years in Edmonton before his trade to the Kings and now felt a special excitement surge through his body as he skated onto the ice for the pregame warm-up.

Wearing a Kings uniform, Gretzky turned more fans on to hockey in Los Angeles.

Gretzky was now the "enemy" in Edmonton, wearing the silver and black of the visiting Kings.

A buzz surged through the crowd as Gretzky took the ice. They had not forgotten The Great One in Edmonton. Soon after his trade, a statue of Gretzky had been erected outside the Northlands Coliseum.

Early in the first period, Gretzky assisted on a goal to tie Howe's record. The fans roared with delight, one of the rare times a visiting player was cheered.

Edmonton goaltender Bill Ranford stopped Gretzky on two good shots in the second period. When Gretzky suffered a bump on the head, he was taken out of the game because of dizziness.

With two minutes to go in the third period, Gretzky missed getting an assist when Ranford stopped another Kings' shot. It didn't look like this would be *the* night.

The Oilers led by one goal with less than a minute left.

Gretzky was on the left side of the net.

"I don't know what made me go there, I'm usually the outlet guy (in the back of the net)," Gretzky said.

Suddenly, a shot hit a teammate and deflected onto his stick. Using Howe's recommended backhand, Gretzky snapped the puck into the net with 53 seconds left.

Howe's record was history.

The Coliseum erupted into cheers after Gretzky's game-tying shot sailed into the net. The game was stopped for a brief ceremony.

What more could Gretzky do that night?

With 1 minute and 36 seconds left in overtime, Gretzky scored the game-winner to give Los Angeles a 5–4 victory.

It was quite a finish. Not only did he break Howe's record, he did it in Edmonton against his former teammates.

It was more memorable than his first return to Edmonton. That night, a tight Gretzky had played a below average game as the Kings lost.

Gretzky's destiny always seemed linked to Edmonton in one way or another. When he returned to play in the 1989 All-Star Game, he won his second All-Star Most Valuable Player Award.

Despite all of Gretzky's accomplishments, he still had dreams. Even though he had broken Howe's points record, Gretzky desperately wanted to break Howe's NHL career goal mark and he wanted to lead the Los Angeles Kings to the Stanley Cup finals.

Not even the Great Gretzky could envision the obstacles he would have to overcome.

Chapter 6

Wayne Gretzky, The Great One, was scared—more scared than he had ever been in his life. The opponent wasn't a hockey team. The opponent was unknown.

This is the way it happened: Gretzky had come to 1992 training camp in top condition and felt fine.

Then disaster struck.

Gretzky was sound asleep. Suddenly he was jolted awake in the middle of the night by a sharp pain in his chest. Frightened, he rushed to the hospital.

The doctors said he had a herniated disk in his back.

Doctors couldn't even speculate when Gretzky would be back on the ice. They had never known an athlete to recover from such an injury.

The Kings' training camp was blanketed with gloom.

Gretzky was in deep despair.

Back injuries are common in hockey. They have shortened many players' careers. Mike Bossy, one of the game's greatest scorers with the New York Islanders, was forced to retire early because of back problems.

For the first time in his life, Gretzky began to have doubts he would ever play hockey again. He was not able to walk without pain: Many days, he found it difficult to stand erect, or hold his children in his arms.

Medical treatment began to reduce the swelling.

"The day the pain stopped is the day I became determined to come back," Gretzky said.

Every day, he worked hard at exercises to improve his back. Every day, he got a little better.

"Hockey has been my life since I was six," Gretzky said. "I was scared of how much I missed it. I was scared by how much I wanted to play."

It was first expected Gretzky would be lost for the season. But he was way ahead of schedule, surprising even himself.

"I could see the fire in his eyes," his wife, Janet, said.

Gretzky could feel the fire in his belly.

"I've always been motivated from within," he said. "I've always had to prove myself. I really push myself to prove people wrong.

"My whole career, I've had to do that. I was 'too small' when I was 10. I was 'too slow' when I was 17. I really wasn't a great player until I won a Cup. . . . "

Doctors had warned Gretzky that a further injury could cripple him for life. But for Wayne Gretzky, there was no life without hockey.

Gretzky, who hadn't played a game since April 28, began skating on December 7. He had his first skate with the Kings on December 26.

"He came determined every day, with a purpose every day," Kings assistant coach Cap Raeder said of Gretzky's skating practices. "It was like he was desperate."

On January 6, 1993, Gretzky was ready to play in a regular-season game. He had missed thirty-nine games before

Wayne Gretzky never gives up. Even after he was diagnosed with a herniated disk in his back, he was able to motivate himself to get onto the ice again.

making his reappearance against the Tampa Bay Lightning at the Los Angeles Forum.

Of all the games in Wayne Gretzky's National Hockey League career, number 1,000 ranked as one of the most memorable. It wasn't the landmark number that was so important. It was the fact he was skating at all. Some considered it a medical miracle.

Gretzky wasn't at his best. But more importantly, he was back on the ice, giving an inspirational lift to his teammates.

At the All-Star Game a month later, Gretzky struggled in the skills competition. He wasn't skating well. The crowd at the Montreal Forum groaned when he slipped on the ice during the puck-carrying race. He was close to quitting.

"I was near the bottom," he said. "I did some soul-searching between periods. What kept me going was one thing my father drilled into us as kids, that what we started we had to finish. I didn't want to quit on myself or on him, so I decided to keep going."

Gretzky continued in a slump. By the time February rolled around, he was saddled with a 16-game goalless streak—the longest of his career by 7 games.

Would the Great Gretzky ever be the same again?

In the middle of February, he started feeling more like himself. He broke out with one goal and four assists in a 10–5 victory over Minnesota.

Gretzky was back!

It couldn't have come at a better time for the Kings. The playoffs loomed ahead and a healthy Gretzky could make all the difference in the world.

At the start of the season, the Kings were not rated among the NHL's elite teams. But they looked elite as they advanced through the playoffs.

Gretzky wasn't able to play as well as he had in the past when he returned to the ice after his medical problems. In February 1993, however, the old Gretzky was back! He scored a goal and had four assists in the Kings' victory over Minnesota.

First they beat Calgary, then Vancouver. Both were considered upsets.

In the conference finals, the Kings faced a powerful Toronto team.

The series was exciting and excruciating. Gretzky was criticized for uneven play as the Kings fell behind the Maple Leafs, 3 games to 2.

Gretzky scored the overtime game-winner in Game Six to tie the series. He then scored three goals as Los Angeles won Game Seven.

The Kings were in the finals for the first time in their history. Their opponents were the Montreal Canadiens.

The first two games of the finals were at the Montreal Forum. Winning at the Forum was always a difficult feat for visiting teams.

Yet the Kings won the opening game in Montreal and were on their way to winning the second game. They led 2–1 with less then two minutes left.

Success was within the Kings' grasp, when suddenly the game was stopped.

Montreal coach Jacques Demers was waving wildly from the Canadiens' bench and pointing.

The fans in the Montreal Forum were puzzled. What was going on?

Officials came and took Kings forward Marty McSorley's hockey stick over to the boards to examine it.

Then everyone knew.

Demers had noticed McSorley using a stick that seemed to be curved more than the legal limit. With his team trailing by one goal and time running out, it was as good a time as any to call him on it.

The stick was illegal.

McSorley was sent to the penalty box, leaving the Kings

short a man. Now the Canadiens were on a power play. They had one more skater on the ice and a better chance of scoring.

The Canadiens quickly cashed in to tie the game and won in overtime, 3–2.

The curved-stick incident turned the series around. The Canadiens won the next three games to gain the Cup.

At the end, Gretzky was exhausted, both physically and mentally. He had played inspirational hockey throughout the series. And now, he considered his future in the gloom and doom of the Kings' locker room.

Suddenly, he felt old. He said he was thinking about retirement. He was only thirty-two, but the playoffs had taken an emotional toll on him.

During the summer he had a change of heart and signed a new three-year contract worth about $25 million.

At the end of the 1993 season, when the Kings lost the Stanley Cup finals to the Canadiens, Gretzky considered retirement. Though he was only thirty-two, the loss had taken a huge emotional and physical drain on him.

Gretzky again broke a record by Gordie Howe when he scored the 802nd goal of his NHL career. Whereas it had taken Howe 26 seasons to score 801 goals, Gretzky broke the record in only 15 seasons.

Gretzky began the 1993–94 season with renewed motivation. His main goal was to lead the Kings back to the Stanley Cup finals. But he also had other goals—actually 37.

That's the number he needed to break the NHL career goal record of 801 by Gordie Howe.

Gretzky had a good chance to break Howe's record, his last major goal, in the 1993–94 season.

Gretzky was right on schedule. He had 799 goals in the books when he faced the San Jose Sharks in a road game on March 20, 1994.

He scored once. Then he scored again to tie Howe's record as the Kings tied the Sharks, 6–6.

The next goal would be the recordbreaker.

The Kings were playing the Vancouver Canucks at home.

For the first period, Gretzky was held scoreless.

With less than six minutes remaining in the second period, Gretzky and McSorley, his old teammate from Edmonton, staged a classic give-and-go. Skating down the ice, Gretzky passed the puck to McSorley—then headed straight for the left circle.

"When I gave the puck to Marty, I knew that he would somehow try to give it back to me," Gretzky said.

He did. Gretzky took the cross-ice pass and fired a wrist shot past goaltender Kirk McLean, who had been pulled out of position by McSorley skating down the right side.

Goal number 802 was in the books!

The recordbreaker set off pandemonium in the L.A. Forum. Gretzky's teammates dashed off the bench to congratulate him. The sellout crowd of 16,005 was on its feet, shouting, "Gretzky . . . Gretzky . . . Gretzky!"

Gretzky's first thought was of his father. He skated over to the stands to whisper something in his ear.

Walter Gretzky had suffered a brain aneurism (blood clot)

Gretzky has dominated the hockey world like no other. His involvement in the sport is directly related to expansion teams in Florida and California, as well as the change in hockey's overall image.

two years before. He was now back on his feet and almost back to his usual self. Sitting with Gretzky's father were his mother, Phyllis, wife Janet, and his three children—Paulina, Ty, and Trevor.

There was a brief ceremony at center ice. Film footage of the careers of Gretzky and Howe was flashed on the replay screen. It had taken Howe 26 seasons to score 801 goals. Gretzky broke the record in 15 seasons.

It was Gretzky's 61st record. And because Gordie Howe was his boyhood hero and longtime friend, the most personal of all.

Gretzky's life had flashed through his mind after scoring the milestone goal: " . . . my dad's illness, the four Stanley Cups in Edmonton, all the bad and good things that have happened to me. Tonight, the excitement, the emotion, the relief . . . it was tough times getting to this point."

Gretzky could have been thinking of the time he was rejected for his first hockey team . . . the jealous parents in Brantford . . . losing three front teeth as a teenager . . . leaving home at the age of fourteen to play in Toronto . . . finding the courage to play when he was the youngest and smallest . . . the struggles with the Indianapolis Racers . . . the shocking trade to Los Angeles . . . and the fear he would never play hockey again because of his back injury.

With his tenth scoring championship in fourteen years, Gretzky was dominating his era much like Babe Ruth had dominated baseball in the 1920s. And like Ruth, Gretzky had raised the awareness of his sport.

For many years, hockey had just been a regional, cold-weather sport. The NHL had hoped Wayne Gretzky's move to Los Angeles would open expansion possibilities on the West Coast.

It did that—and more.

Soon, two new teams sprang up in California, two in Florida, and one moved south to Texas as warm-weather sites suddenly became hot spots for NHL teams in the nineties.

Gretzky had already put Edmonton on the hockey map. Now he was lifting a league to a new level of popularity in the United States.

As he makes his way to the Hockey Hall of Fame, Gretzky has set standards that will be hard to equal by future generations. But his uniqueness and impact cannot be measured by mere statistics.

With his creativity and nonviolent approach, he has helped to change hockey's image from a rough sport to a skilled sport. He takes his role seriously as a model for youngsters and is the number one ambassador for his sport. He is always patient and well-mannered on and off the ice.

Wayne Gretzky will always be known as "The Great One" for what he has done for the game of hockey.

Career Statistics

Season	Team	League	GP	G	A	PTS	PIM
1979-80	Edmonton	NHL	79	51	86	137	21
1980-81	Edmonton	NHL	80	55	109	164	28
1981-82	Edmonton	NHL	80	92	120	212	26
1982-83	Edmonton	NHL	80	71	125	196	59
1983-84	Edmonton	NHL	74	87	118	205	39
1984-85	Edmonton	NHL	80	73	135	208	52
1985-86	Edmonton	NHL	80	52	163	215	46
1986-87	Edmonton	NHL	79	62	121	183	28
1987-88	Edmonton	NHL	64	40	109	149	24
1988-89	Los Angeles	NHL	78	54	114	168	26
1989-90	Los Angeles	NHL	73	40	102	142	42
1990-91	Los Angeles	NHL	78	41	122	163	16
1991-92	Los Angeles	NHL	74	31	90	121	34
1992-93	Los Angeles	NHL	45	16	49	65	6
1993-94	Los Angeles	NHL	81	38	92	130	20
1994-95	Los Angeles	NHL	48	11	37	48	6
NHL Totals			1173	814	1692	2506	473

GP=Games Played   PTS=Total Goals and Assists
G=Goals Scored   PIM=Penalty in Minutes
A=Assists

Where to Write Wayne Gretzky

Mr. Wayne Gretzky
c/o Los Angeles Kings
The Great Western Forum
P.O. Box 17013
Inglewood, CA 90308

Index

New York Islanders, 25, 27, 29, 45, 49
Nith River, 15
Northlands Coliseum, 45, 46

P

Patrick, Steve, 9
Philadelphia Flyers, 31, 32
Pocklington, Peter, 23, 38
Potvin, Denis, 27

R

Raeder, Cap, 50
Ranford, Bill, 47
Ruth, Babe, 25, 59

S

Sather, Glen, 22, 23
Sault Ste. Marie Greyhounds, 18, 19
San Jose Sharks, 57
Smith, Billy, 27
Smith, Steve, 33, 35

Stanley Cup, 25, 29, 30, 33, 35, 36, 38, 40, 48, 57, 59
Stapleton, Pat "Whitey," 22
Stefan, Greg, 43

T

Tampa Bay Lightning, 52
Taylor, Dave, 43
Toronto Young Nationals, 18
Trottier, Bryan, 27

V

Vancouver Canucks, 57
Vernon, Mike, 36

W

World Hockey Association (WHA), 20, 23, 24

Z

Ziegler, John, 9